Creating a Learning University

One Leader's Way of Pursuing Clarity Through Instructional Leadership Team (ILT) Meetings

Dedication

*To my wife, **Felicia**, your love steadies my heart, your faith anchors my purpose, and your quiet strength reminds me daily that leadership begins at home.*

*To our sons, **Jayden, Jacob, and Caleb,** may you live with clarity, lead with compassion, and carry the fire of purpose wherever you go.*

*To my mother, **Sarah Shaw**, who believed in the dream before anyone else could see it.*

*To my **First Missionary Baptist Church of Tuscumbia** family, thank you for your prayers, your faith, and your trust. You remind me that spiritual leadership is still sacred work.*

*To my **Florence City Schools** family, thank you for the lessons that helped me grow, mature e, and see with clarity.*

*To **My Foxhole Friends**, your friendship, partnership, professionalism, grace, trust, truth-telling, and love made the work possible and made me a leader.*

*And to my coach, **Dr. Pete Gorman**, thank you for teaching me that disciplined reflection is a form of love and that systems done well can change lives.*

Table of Contents

Dedication
Preface — Why This Book Exists

Preface

There comes a point in every leader's journey when the meetings, the mandates, and the memos start to sound the same. When you can predict the excuses for why we didn't do what we said we would do. When "accountability" becomes a word people dodge instead of a practice they embrace.

That's where I found myself years ago. I was having another meeting about change; staring at another agenda, another data set, another set of "next steps," wondering if any more than a few people in the room *believed* that what we were trying to do would change our district. Did they think it was possible to improve our district or were we destined to be a respectable B district? I mean, that is good *for a district like yours*. What they really mean is that is *the best you can do with those kids and those families*. I believed in my soul that we were the professionals. We were blessed with several educators with higher degrees. We have great families. We have a history of good educational structures. Yes, I believe that my children have the ability and the right to be their highest and truest selves, not what the socioeconomic heat maps say they are destined to be.

It wasn't that the people weren't working hard. It was that they were just doing school instead of working on the work. We were perfunctory in our work, completing tasks with little collective fire. This was during COVID, so we can all imagine the mindsets that abounded circa 2021.

What was missing wasn't intelligence or heart. What was missing was clarity and collective efficacy. When you don't know exactly what you're chasing, every action feels like movement, but it isn't. Clarity names the destination and dignifies the process. It gives people a clear picture of the impact they have on student learning, as well as all that my colleagues and I are doing that is worthy of celebration.

As a school superintendent and a pastor, I had the unique vantage point of leading both a district and a congregation. I've seen what happens when purpose is clear, and what happens when it's not. In both the classroom and the church house, clarity is the difference between chaos and calling.

This book is about building what I call the *Learning University*. What is that? It is a culture where learning isn't a seasonal initiative but a spiritual discipline; where leaders are students first, and every meeting is a classroom.

It's also about a framework, *CRT-CM*, that helped us move from confusion to clarity; from clarity to accountability; from accountability to transformation:

- **Clarity**: naming what we're really after.
- **Resources**: equipping the work we claim to value.
- **Training**: ensuring consistency over charisma. All surrounded by **Coaching and Monitoring,** the continuous circle that keeps it alive.

The goal isn't perfection. It is the pursuit of the highest and truest you as you walk this journey. The journey matters more than the destination because it takes each person higher and closer to their truest self.

If we can pursue the clarity of purpose together, in classrooms, churches, and communities, then maybe, just maybe, our students, our teachers, and our families will begin to see that leadership is less about control and more about cultivation.

This book is for every leader who knows the weight of responsibility and the whisper of purpose.

- For the ones trying to turn meetings into movements.
- For the ones trying to keep the faith while facing the brutal facts.
- For those who refuse to let any mission that God puts them on lose its soul.

May these pages give you pause, make you think deeper about what is in your soul, and lead you more courageously.

Because clarity, once found, changes everything. Clarity leads to accountability. Accountability leads to transformation. Personal transformation leads to organizational transformation.

Jimmy D. Shaw Jr., Ed.D.
Florence, Alabama

Introduction

Learning University? Why & So What?

The phrase *"Learning University"* came to me one afternoon while sitting with some colleagues at a professional development session at an out-of-state university. We were knee-deep in spreadsheets, data, and questions about where we were going next. As we talked about student learning, it dawned upon me that students don't learn if they are not in an atmosphere of learning. If learning is not in the dust, the dirt, the air; if learning so that you can help others to learn is not the very purpose of the organization, then for most people, it won't happen; for the adults or the children.

The irony was painful. We were educational leaders, but we weren't learning. As my friend Dr. Jackie Flowers says, we were trying to do something **to** teachers rather than **becoming** and embodying what we wanted to see in them.

That realization led to a single question that changed the rhythm of our work:

> "What would it look like if our district became a learning university? What if we were a place where learning never stops, for anyone, adult or child?"

That question sparked a vision, which became our purpose.

Purpose

To effectively advance learning and opportunities for all students to achieve and grow, we will create a *Learning University* at both the district and school levels. This university will have a clear standard for what happens in a teaching and learning culture by focusing on model practices that can be implemented, replicated, assessed, and monitored by district and school teams.

Our outcomes will be driven by three pillars:

1. Culture – what we will no longer tolerate.
2. Practices – what we expect to see consistently happening.
3. Student Achievement – the ultimate measure of how our practices impact children.

This isn't just a plan for education. This is a blueprint for leadership.

When culture, practice, and accountability align for the same purpose, clarity is the offspring. When clarity is present, organizations become more functional because the what and the why are made plain. Once clarity arrives, the organization can become fiercely, truthfully, and collaboratively because we build the how.

Desired Outcomes

Our aim is to advance how we build capacity in school leadership teams: principals, assistant principals, instructional coaches/partners, and academic coaches, and to establish exemplars of leadership practice.

We want adult behavior to have a clear through-line to student achievement, from the superintendent's desk to the student's desk:

Superintendent → Principal → Assistant Principal → Coach → Academic Lead → Teacher → Student.

Everyone must see themselves in the work that supports the vision.

When leaders understand that alignment, the conversation shifts. We stop asking *"Who's responsible?"* and start asking, *"Who owns it?"* That's how we turn leadership teams into learning teams.

The Discipline of Reflection: Dr. Shaw's ILT Questions

In the Learning University, we don't move by feelings. We act after monitoring and then reflecting upon what we saw. To get to a plan of attack, we must build the body of our plan. The following questions became the backbone of our ILTs:

1. **Why?** What statistical data led you to this? What is your fire?
2. **What?** What is the goal: the destination?
3. **How?** How will you get there?
4. **How to define success?** – What evidence will show it's working?
5. **How to measure it?** – What tools will you use to monitor progress?

6. **How to communicate it?** – Who needs to know and how?
7. **How will you celebrate it?** – How will you acknowledge the wins?
8. **What is the through line?** – Name the people; clarify the ownership.

Each question pushes leaders beyond compliance into consciousness. You can't transform what you refuse to examine. You cannot make it to a destination until you are willing to clearly define where you are, where you're going, and what the checkpoints are along the way. Reflection is not the break from the work; it *is* the work. The destination is a byproduct of the journey.

Why the CRT-CM Framework Matters

The CRT-CM Framework: Clarity, Resources, Training, surrounded by Coaching and Monitoring, became the framework that held all of this together. It's both a diagnostic and a discipline: a way of checking if your system is healthy and a process for making it healthier.

- **Clarity** defines the vision.
- **Resources** provide all the needed tools to accomplish the mission.
- **Training** is preparation we must provide for the team to be successful with the right action, done in the most effective way for you.
- **Coaching and Monitoring** legitimize the learning process.

When one piece fails, the culture falters. When all are aligned, the organization's movement makes its own concerto.

Why a Learning University?

In short, everyone is a learner. How do we equip the principal teachers to be the principal learners to get better? The dream is that every school, every department, every classroom, becomes part of the Learning University. A living, breathing ecosystem of shared goals, best practices for their situation, and growth as an organizational nonnegotiable for everyone. Where leaders model being a lead learner for the adults, and adults' model being a voracious learner for students and each other, curiosity, humility, efficacy, and perseverance grow.

The Learning University isn't a program. It is a system of problem-solving, communication, and growth. It's a daily decision to take life and learn from every failure and celebrate every victory of learning progress. So, before we talk about systems and strategies, let's talk about *sight*. Because if we can't see clearly, we can't lead wisely.

And that bring us to Chapter 1

Clarity: The North Star of the Work.

Chapter 1

Clarity: The North Star of the Work

1. The Power of Vision

Every strong organization begins with a shared vision, but a shared vision means nothing if it's blurry. Clarity is the light that cuts through the fog. It tells everyone, *"This is where we are. This is where we're headed."*

Before we ever talk about initiatives or improvement plans, the first responsibility of leadership is to *see*, and then to *help others see.*

Clarity is not complicated language or long documents. It is the simple, sober articulation of what matters most. It answers the question: *If our students are to win this year, what piece of student data will we use to measure progress and how much progress will mean success?*

When a leader gains clarity, direction stops being optional. People can handle hard work, but they can't overcome a lack of vision. Clarity is essential.

2. Clarity in the Classroom and the Church

I've watched teachers lose heart because expectations shifted with every new initiative. I've watched congregations shrink because of extreme change and lack thereof. In both spaces, the issue wasn't effort; it was a lack of clarity about where they were, where they were going, and why.

In my school system and at my church, I discovered that clarity has two sides:

1.   The organizational side, what we do.
2.   The spiritual side, why we do it.

When both sides align, work becomes worship. Every lesson plan, every sermon, every meeting becomes an offering of excellence unto God.

Dr. Gardner Taylor once said, *"There's nothing worse than a fog in the pulpit."* There's also nothing worse than a fog in leadership. When the leader's vision or direction is unclear, the people wander. When the leader is clear in where they are, where they are going, and why, even the weary can walk by faith.

3. What Clarity Looks Like

Clarity shows up when:

- The vision is short enough to repeat and strong enough to sustain.
- The goals connect directly to student growth.
- Every meeting has a stated purpose and a defined product.
- People can finish the sentence, *"We are doing this because..."*

Clarity is also measurable. In our district, we began defining clarity with the same precision we used for test data. We didn't guess about clarity; we checked for it. When we fell short, we didn't blame; we looked at our process data, we revisited, refocused, and restated until everyone could see it.

4. The Process of Naming

I often remind my ILT: *If you can't name it, you can't change it.* Naming gives power. In Genesis, God gave Adam the authority to name creation. Every name carried identity and purpose.

Leadership does the same. When you name the priority-reading fluency, positive culture, equitable discipline- you give it permission to exist and demand it to be addressed. You give wayward souls a direction.

That's why clarity isn't about charisma; it's about courage. It takes courage to name what's broken and call everyone to address it.

5. Clarity and the CRT-CM Framework

Clarity is the first letter for a reason; it drives the rest.

- Without **clarity**, resources are scattered.
- Without **clarity**, training is inconsistent.
- Without **clarity**, coaching and monitoring become guesswork.

The triangle begins at "C" because clarity points the direction of every line that follows. It is the North Star that aligns the system.

Every week, our ILT would start with one question:

> *"What is the goal? What are we working on? Where are we according to the data?"*

Sometimes it was instruction. Sometimes communication. Sometimes expectations. But always clarity first.

6. When Clarity Is Missing

Lack of clarity breeds noise: endless meetings, circular conversations, defensive emails. People fill the silence with assumption. That's when the mission starts to drift and morale begins to sink.

When we found ourselves there, we didn't schedule more meetings. We went back to *why*. We read the vision statement aloud. We reminded one another what success would look like for children who can't yet speak for themselves.

Clarity always brings you back to the purpose, the people.

7. Spiritual Clarity

Clarity is not just strategic, it's sacred. Jesus never left His followers guessing. He said, *"I am the way, the truth, and the life."* (John 14:6 NKJV) He gave direction before departure, promise before pain. As leaders, we are stewards of that same responsibility. We owe our people truth spoken plainly, purpose stated simply, and expectations explained patiently.

When the work gets heavy, clarity keeps you from quitting because it keeps the vision ever before you. It is your light on the hill. Because when you know where you're going and why you're going, you can endure almost any "how."

8. Reflection Prompts: Questions to Consider

Why? What data revealed that there is a problem?

What? What do we want to do about it?

How? How will you communicate and model that plan?

How to address it? How will you respond if clarity slips?

How to define success? What adult actions do we believe will lead to student learning evidence that will signify success?

How to communicate it? Who needs to hear it, from whom, and how often?

How to measure it? How will you measure student progress and/or what tool will you use to monitor clearly defined adult behaviors?

How will you celebrate it? Because clarity led to transformation, how will you honor impactful and consistent action?

Who will own it? Everyone must see themselves, clearly, in the work.

ILT Reflection Sheet — Clarity Focus

Closing Thought

Clarity doesn't make leadership easier. It makes it *possible*. Once you name what matters and your current state, everything else either moves us closer to the goal or distracts us from it. When we lead with clarity, people don't just follow instructions; they can be freed to act with conviction.

> **Clarity is the first act of leadership.**
> **Everything else follows it.**

Chapter 2

Resources: Fuel for the Fire

1. The Principle of Provision

You can't expect results from a plan you never equip for success. Vision without provision is just frustration dressed up as leadership, or as they used to say when I was a younger man, plans with no money mean you're just selling dreams.

Once clarity names the destination, resources pack the car for the trip. Every system, school, church, or district needs fuel, drivers, luggage, and a map or a phone with a digital map to move from aspiration to action. Resources aren't just money. Resources are time, tools, people, spaces, and trust. In education, we often shout expectations from the mountaintop but send our teams into the valley empty-handed, with some tools but not enough to get the job done.

If the mission is worth doing, it's worth resourcing, or as my mother would say, ALL THE TIME, "A job worth doing is worth doing well." There is no reason to half-do a job. Samson killed thousands of his enemies with the jawbone of an ass. Sometimes we send people out without even that. We must give people something to fight with.

The Apostle Paul told the Corinthians that *"He who sows sparingly will also reap sparingly."* (2 Corinthians 9:6

NKJV) The same is true in leadership. You can't sow scarcity and expect to harvest excellence. It's not always more money. Sometimes it is being creative with how you schedule so that teachers can have an extra time per day to have Common Planning Time (CPTs; our version of a PLC). It might be finding the most closely aligned diagnostic so that your schools can have peace of mind that when they take the time to stop giving instruction to give a diagnostic, they can know it is as closely aligned to the state summative assessments as possible.

2. Understanding What Counts as a Resource

Leaders often think resources mean dollars and cents. But the most valuable resources are often invisible:

- A well-designed schedule that gives teachers time to collaborate.
- A data dashboard that shows patterns before they become problems.
- A mentor teacher who can also coach instead of criticizing.
- A culture where questions are welcomed, not weaponized.
- A well-defined meeting structure prevents wasting time.
- A well-designed, embedded professional development structure

A good leader identifies resources others overlook. Jesus fed five thousand people not because He had more bread, but because He had more faith in what was already in His hands.

Sometimes your greatest resource is what you've been ignoring.

3. Aligning Resources to Priorities

During my time as a superintendent, I learned that every budget line is tied to a story. If the story didn't match our stated goals, something had to change.

When we said literacy was our priority, we made sure the funding, training, and time allocation reflected that. When we said empowering students was our commitment, we funded interventions that matched our conviction.

Budgets and calendars are moral documents. They reveal what you value. Alignment is the greatest multiplier. When resources flow in the same direction as clarity, progress becomes inevitable.

4. People as Resources

Money can buy materials, but it can't buy momentum. People create that.

I've seen districts spend thousands on programs that collect dust because they didn't invest in training the people who had to implement them. A trained, trusted, and empowered teacher is more powerful than any software subscription.

That's why in the Learning University; every person is seen as both a contributor and a capacity-builder. Our best resource isn't what's in the curriculum hub; it's who's in the room.

When you treat people as partners instead of placeholders, they start leading instead of waiting to be led.

5. The Spiritual Side of Resourcing

In ministry, I learned that provision always follows purpose. When God gives vision, He supplies what the vision requires.

That principle holds true in leadership. If you're operating within your purpose, the right resources will arrive, but they often come in the form of responsibility first.

Gideon didn't get more soldiers; he got clarity of calling. David didn't need Saul's armor; he needed courage to use his sling. Provision follows purpose, but purpose must be clear enough for people to rally behind.

6. A Case Study: The Reading Renaissance

At one of our elementary schools, reading proficiency was stagnant. We had data, but no direction.

Clarity: We named the goal, 85% of students reading on grade level by spring.

Resources: We assigned reading coaches to work with each grade band on what solid structures and processes should be present for good, connected small-group stations, and how we should help implement those.

Training: We made time for every elementary teacher who was a core teacher to have two CPTs per week by adding extra specials in the schedule. During this time, one CPT a week was dedicated to common lesson planning and the other was dedicated to data analysis.

Coaching & Monitoring: We tracked reading growth every week based on Common Formative Assessments (CFAs) and publicly celebrated progress. Within one year, proficiency rose six points on the state report card and a double-digit gain in student growth and achievement in reading and ELA. The difference wasn't a new program; it was the clarity of a plan of attack and the way the team was able to shift resources to what they felt mattered most.

7. The Resource Audit

Every leadership team should regularly ask:

1. Do our resources reflect our goals and priorities?
2. Are we investing in people or just purchases?
3. What do we already have that we're not using well?
4. Who controls resources that could be shared?
5. What small thing can we do to unleash the latent potential of our people?

A curriculum and resource audit doesn't just save money; it reveals alignment of mission, vision, and resources.

8. Application: Resourcing the ILT

Your Instructional Leadership Team is the engine of the Learning University, and engines need maintenance. Whenever the ILT decides on a goal and direction, we conduct an ILT Resource Review. This practice forced us to lead from vision instead of tradition. We stopped saying "we can't afford it" and started asking "can we afford not to?"

9. Reflection Prompts

1. What key priorities in your school or district are currently under-resourced? In other words, are you putting your money where your mouth is?
2. Which existing resources are being underused because of unclear direction?
3. How does your budget or calendar reflect what you say you value?
4. How are you resourcing people, not just programs?
5. What small reallocation could make a big difference?

10. ILT Reflection Sheet — Resource Focus

Question

What?

What specific resources are required to meet the goal?

How?

How will you allocate or reallocate them?

How to address it?

What will you do if the resource plan doesn't work?

How to define success?

What measurable change will prove resources were used effectively?

How to communicate it?

Who must be informed and how?

How to measure it?

How will you monitor resource use and impact?

How will you celebrate it?

How will you honor those who maximized what they had?

Who will do what?

Does everyone see themselves in the work?

Closing Thought

Resources don't create success; their alignment to purpose does. When you lead with clarity, every dollar, every hour, and every effort falls into alignment. That's when good systems become great ones.

"You cannot give what you do not have."

Chapter 3

Training: The Engine of Consistency

1. Training Is How Vision Becomes Habit

Once clarity gives direction and resources provide support, training turns theory into muscle memory. Training is the bridge between what people *know* and what they do.

Every organization, whether a school district or a church, has moments when leaders assume everyone already knows what to do. That assumption is how excellence erodes. If consistency is the goal, training is the engine. Practice makes permanent.

You cannot expect precision without preparation. You cannot expect execution without equipment.

A good coach would never throw a team onto the field without practice. A good pastor would never send out a minister without prior preparation on how to handle himself or herself in someone else's pulpit. Yet too often, leaders hand out mandates with no modeling. Training ensures that people don't just understand the "what," but also the "how."

2. Training as a Form of Love

Training isn't control; it's care. When you take the time to train people well, you're telling them, *"I believe in your ability to grow."* Training is leadership through proximity. It says, "I'll walk beside you, not stand in front of you, and bark orders."

Jesus trained His disciples by doing, explaining, modeling, answering their questions, and then He sent them. He didn't simply command; He demonstrated. When He fed the multitude, He showed them how to organize the crowd. When He healed, He let them see His compassion, His why, then He showed them what to do and how to do it. When He sent them out, He equipped them with both message and method. He told them what to do when they were welcomed, and He told them what to do when the mission was going to fail. When Jesus trained, He spoke truth, then He modeled for them, so it was not just theory, but they had a chance to see it done in action. He was beside them, not in a half-day training, and then sent them out into the field. Teaching is training, and training is a contact sport.

3. The Model: Training that Sticks

During this time, we realized that the quality of professional development was only as strong as its follow-through and its ability to have ongoing coaching and feedback. So, we redesigned our approach.

We stopped having "one-shot" or quarterly professional development without systemic follow-through. We started prioritizing embedded professional development because training wasn't an event; it was a part of a learning cycle, an evolution that led to improvement of practice, teaching, and learning. In the words of the great Paul Bambrick-Santoyo, we wanted to "Get Better, Faster," but in the context of the venerable Dr. Jackie Walsh and Cathy Gassenhimer, "sometimes you have to go slow to go fast."

Professional development that sticks has three key principles:

1. **Model It.** Let participants see it done right before they're asked to do it.
2. **Motivate It** Practice in a safe space, with feedback, because practice does not make perfect. Practice makes permanent.
3. **Measure It.** Have clear measures for action and follow-up to ensure transfer from practice to application is happening and how it's happening.

When we shifted from presentation to presentation and practice, real learning and change occurred. People began to replicate excellence instead of working themselves tirelessly for the same results, not knowing why their effort was not having the impact. Training is not about more information; it's about more clarity of the standard. Once everyone knows what it is supposed to look like, then they are better able to articulate what changes could have the greatest impact. As author Jocko Willink said, "There is freedom within form."

4. How Training Connects to the CRT-CM Framework

The CRT-CM Framework reminds us that clarity and resources mean nothing without training.

- **Clarity** defines what you expect.
- **Resources** provide what you need.
- **Training** ensures everyone is empowered to execute.
- **Coaching & Monitoring** sustain it.

Training is the hinge point where the plan meets the people. It's the step that turns mission statements into daily routines. It is the show of what. We always tell people what we want. We will even show them what it looks like as a finished product. But when people fail, it is often the case that we have not trained them.

If Clarity is the North Star, Training is the compass. It keeps everyone moving in the right direction, no matter the obstacles.

5. Training is Culture, not a Calendar

We began teaching our leaders that training isn't an event that happens because it's a Professional Development (PD) Day. PD is what happens *because* of the calendar. I am a firm believer in the old adage that there are two documents that show you who you are and what you believe in any organization. Those two are the calendar and the budget. If you love it enough to budget money for it, if you find it valuable enough to publicly say that we are GOING TO spend time doing it, then what is contained in the budget and on the calendar becomes a piece of the culture, not an event.

Every ILT meeting became a mini lab. Every CPT became a micro-university. A study of action. Instead of sending memos, we had principal meetings once a month at the school site. Why? Because looking at the actionable things happening in every school was a part of a learning university culture. ILTs and principal meetings at the school allowed us to see the theory in action and the action applied to our students, in our culture.

Teachers stopped waiting for workshops because training was now embedded in the workday. That is learning and growing and coaching at its finest. That's when culture shifted, when learning by doing became the norm, not the novelty.

6. The Consistency Equation

Inconsistent outcomes are always a training issue. If ten teachers hear one message ten different ways, the problem isn't their ears: it's your process. Group training equalizes opportunity. It ensures that success isn't dependent on who's in the room, but on what's been reinforced in the system. It increases common language and common commitment to the work. That's why I began every semester with a formula that would create consistency. As the old saying goes, practice makes permanent.

Consistency = Clarity × Training × Follow-Through

It was a reminder that even great vision will fail if the people carrying it aren't trained the same way, hear the same language, and are asked to apply their theories to action, in their environment, and then monitor it. That is how you get consistent receipts. Consistency protects clarity from chaos. Chaos makes excuses for results. Consistency imposes its will on a problem and does not allow the problem to be so great that we all look at the problem likes it's the professional rather than us looking at the problem like we are. Problems must change when we all work together to impact them. *Know thy impact.* Together we are strong.

5 Then the Lord came down to look over the city and the tower that the men were building. 6 The Lord said, "If they have begun to do this as one people all having the same language, then nothing they plan to do will be impossible for them. (Genesis 11: 5-6 HCSB)

7. Spiritual Training: The Discipleship Parallel

In ministry, the word *disciple* literally means *apprentice.* Training, therefore, is sacred work. Learning, training, and doing are what transform us. Jesus did not just talk about sacrifice. He DID what He talked about. He sacrificed Himself and went to the cross. Doing is what shapes the learner's soul.

Jesus didn't pick the most polished followers; He picked those willing to be shaped, willing to do. Likewise, leadership is about forming people before you can transform systems. Remember, God created all of us, but some of us He has called to shape and form others into their highest and truest selves. Some leaders have the ability to teach, coach, and mentor. Be obedient to your calling. We can't expect discipleship-level results from drive-through-level training. In education and faith, the mission is too important to leave to guesswork.

8. Application: Building a Training Cycle for the ILT

In the Learning University, every ILT establishes a Training Cycle that follows four stages:

1. **Identify the Gap.** Where are we? What skill or understanding do we think is missing?
2. **Plan the Training.** What model, method, or mentor will fill the gap?
3. **Deliver and practice.** There must be practice in the training, not just talking. You do not fix anything until you do what you say. Doing matters.
4. **Follow Up and Feedback.** Monitor execution. Coach refinement.

9. Reflection Prompts

1. How does your current training culture reinforce or erode consistency?
2. What percentage of your PD results in actual change in classroom practice?
3. Where have you mistaken communication for training?
4. How can you model the behaviors you're asking others to learn?
5. What's one training system you could institutionalize this semester?

10. ILT Reflection Sheet — Training Focus

Question

Why?

What image does the data mirror show you? Where does the data say you are?

What?

What specific training will address the need? What do the experts in the room say needs to happen to improve said data?

How?

How will you design and deliver the training to positively impact the data?

How to define success?

What measurable evidence will confirm learning transfer?

How to communicate it?

How will you share purpose and expectations?

How to measure it?

What ongoing assessments or observations will verify results?

How to address it?

What will you do if results don't show improvement?

How will you celebrate it?

How will you recognize implementation and growth?

Who will do all of this (Through Line)?

Closing Thought

Training doesn't slow down the mission. Show people how you want things done and explain why is about improving and equipping your people. Let them have a voice in this process. Systems and people sustain success, but a team of people that don't have a system will soon leave, and what is left? A well-trained team will produce predictable excellence but with the artistry and the creativity of a master.

When clarity sets the standard and training sets the rhythm, excellence stops being the exception and starts being the expectation.

"Training (Doing) is how vision becomes habit."

Chapter 4

Coaching & Monitoring: The Circle That Keeps It Alive

1. The Living Circle

If clarity points the way, resources are the vehicle to get you there. Training builds the skills, then coaching and monitoring are the crucible and the fire that forge success. They are not punishment; they shape an ordinary hunk of metal into Valyrian Steel. They cannot add. They only bring out the greatness that is already present. Coaching and monitoring answer the questions of how you know and what you are going to do about it. They don't exist to police the work but to progress the work by empowering the Doers of the work.

Every thriving system breathes. Monitoring is the inhale. Monitoring brings insight, clarity, and receipts. Coaching is the exhale. It is the encouragement, support, celebration, accountability, reflection, and results.

Together, they form a continuous rhythm of growth that says, *"We care enough to check on you, and we love enough to support you."*

2. The Misunderstood Twin

Many leaders separate coaching and monitoring, treating one as nurturing and the other as judgmental. But in truth, they are twins born from the same commitment to excellence.

- **Coaching** speaks to people's *potential, what they can be.*
- **Monitoring** speaks to people's *practice. "This is what we saw."*

When we coach without monitoring, we inspire or criticize without evidence.

When we monitor without coaching, we are practicing motion but no movement.

But when we merge the two, we get momentum with meaning.

We used to have meetings where data was the star. Graphs, charts, color codes, all facts, very little belief. Then we started adding coaching questions:

"What do we see happening in the room, the hallways, the small group table?"

"What did you do well? What small, bite-sized adjustment do we need to make?"

"What can we do to make this go from theory to action?"

Suddenly, the data stopped feeling like a diagnosis and started feeling like direction.

3. Coaching as Ministry

In the church, I've learned that preaching changes hearts, but pastoring changes lives. The same is true for leadership. Coaching is the pastoral side of management. It cares for the person while improving the performance. Dr. E.K. Bailey called it "preaching to the potential in people." Coaching is side-by-side action with your team. You must be in the trenches with them to see not only what they are doing, but who they could become. Your next leader is often right there under our noses, if we can only cultivate them. We are the faith that they don't have.

A good coach doesn't just critique; they cultivate. They stand besides, not above.

They remind people that accountability is not aggression; it's affirmation, it is the allegiance that the master is obligated to offer to the pupil to help them get better. It is the actual work that they do that matters, not just talking about the results. If you want somebody to talk to, get a mentor. If you want someone to be honest with you and walk beside you to help you reach the best you, get a coach.

4. Monitoring with Mercy

Monitoring gets a bad reputation because people associate it with surveillance. We used to use terms like "Snoopervision," as if hiding monitoring helped anybody. True monitoring is stewardship. By inspecting what you expect, and then supporting people to help reach that mark, you are honoring the work.

In Scripture, watchmen stood on the walls not to criticize the city but to protect it. Monitoring does the same. It guards the integrity of the work. When we implemented monitoring protocols in Florence, we started by changing our language. It is about getting better. It is formative. Some still did not believe us. But to those who saw their students' learning increase, those understood that we weren't just collecting compliance data; we were cultivating our vision.

When the principals caught that vision. When they began to trust our actions, everything changed. Principals and coaches started inviting us in instead of hiding from walkthroughs. Leaders started asking for feedback instead of fearing it. When monitoring begins to be mentorship and coaching, it multiplies engagement.

5. The Circle in Motion

In the **CRT-CM Framework**, coaching and monitoring form the circle that surrounds the triangle. That circle means continuity, no beginning, no end. It is "the how" of continuous improvement.

- **Clarity** gives direction.
- **Resources** provide tools.
- **Training** builds consistency.
- **Coaching & Monitoring** ensure growth.

A circle means every initiative is revisited, reflected upon, and refined. The work never dies; it evolves.

6. The Florence Feedback Loop

Here's how it looked in practice:

After our reading initiative (see Chapter 2), coaches continued classroom visits. Instead of checking compliance, they used three guiding questions:

1. *What does the data say students need us to focus on?*
2. *What can we do about it?*
3. *What's the next step?*

Teachers began anticipating feedback, not dreading it. Walkthroughs became two-way conversations. And data became a source of celebrations, and not just interrogations.

7. When Coaching and Monitoring Go Wrong

Without clear purpose, coaching and monitoring can become toxic:

- Too much coaching without accountability creates comfort zones.
- Too much monitoring without proper feedback creates fear zones.

The antidote is balance. Coaching must lift. Monitoring must anchor. As leaders, we must remember that people resist feedback because they equate it to subjective humiliation. Our job is to build people, not break them.

8. Spiritual Dimension: The Shepherd's Eye

Jesus modeled the perfect coaching and monitoring relationship with His disciples. He taught, He sent, He watched, He corrected, and He restored. After Peter denied Him, Jesus didn't replace him; He reinstated him. "Feed my sheep," he said (John 21:17). That was both accountability and affirmation.

Leaders, your job isn't just to catch mistakes. It is to improve practice and restore confidence. We are more than supervisors, and they are more than just employees. They are the people who we have been assigned to shepherd, on purpose. When your people know you're watching to help, not to hurt, they will perform with a little less dog and pony and a little more confidence and lift because they are empowered, not afraid.

9. Application: The ILT Coaching & Monitoring Cycle

Each ILT should establish a Coaching & Monitoring Cycle that includes:

1. **Scheduled Meetings.** Regularly timed observations and conversations.
2. **Feedback Framework.** Clear measurement tool with clear focus areas.
3. **Reflective Dialogue.** Start with questions, not conclusions.
4. **Documentation.** Track progress. We used School Mint Grown, formerly known as Whetstone, but you can use Google Forms or anything else.

5. **Celebration.** Celebrate publicly. Reward
    consistency. Coach cantily.

Question

Why?

What data shows a need for coaching or
monitoring?

What?

What will be your coaching and monitoring
focus?

How?

How will you structure time for feedback
conversations (in-the-moment or follow-up
afterwards)?

How to address it?

What will you do if coaching or monitoring isn't
consistent?

How to define success?

What observable changes (receipts) will indicate
growth?

How to communicate it?

How will you share purpose, the feedback process
and the training plan for giving and receiving
feedback?

How to measure it?

How will you monitor if feedback is happening and the
quality of it?

How will you celebrate it?

How will you recognize those who respond well to
coaching?

Who will do all of this? Who will own it?

10. Reflection Prompts

1. How do your teachers and staff currently perceive
   monitoring?
2. What would it take for feedback to feel like a gift
   instead of a curse?
3. How can your ILT demonstrate coaching as
   partnership, not policing?
4. When was the last time you celebrated consistent
   follow-through?

5. What evidence shows coaching and monitoring are alive in your building?

11. ILT Reflection Sheet — Coaching & Monitoring Focus

Closing Thought

Coaching and monitoring are not the end of leadership. They're the residue of its presence. They ensure the song doesn't fade once the meeting ends. When leaders coach with grace and monitor with intention, the system breathes on its own.

> **"Monitoring is the inhale. Coaching is the exhale. Symbiotically, they ensure the life of the pursuit of the goal."**

Chapter 5

The ILT in Motion: Where the Framework Meets the Field

1. From Meeting to Movement

The Instructional Leadership Team (ILT) is where ideas stop being theories and start becoming testimonies. It's the crucible where clarity, resources, training, coaching, and monitoring all meet face to face to produce student success.

A well-led ILT is not a meeting; it's a movement. It's a rhythm of reflection, action, and accountability that breathes life into everything a school touches. It is the Sunday dinner where we all sit down at the table to discuss life, past, present, and future, and decide to make it better.

When I first began observing ILT meetings across our district, I noticed a dangerous trend: we were meeting, but students were not *growing*. There were agendas, but no alignment. Before ILTs, there were one-on-one principal meetings. We were throwing so much at the principal that I am surprised they survived.

That's when I realized: the ILT is not when the staff reports to the principal's office to check one more box. The ILT is the work. When done right, it becomes the clearest mirror of a school's culture: what they want to see happening and what they won't tolerate. Every piece of data that you logged as a fire was something that the ILT said is not acceptable, and we won't tolerate. We're going to do something about it, or fail trying, but talking it to death is not an option.

2. The Rhythm of the Work

An ILT should have a rhythm that mirrors the CRT-CM Framework itself.

Each meeting should include a discussion about:

1. **Clarity:** Identify the focus.
2. **Resources:** What structures and processes are needed?
3. **Training:** Decide, observe, and model what good practice looks like.
4. **Coaching & Monitoring:** What are we looking for, and how will we respond when we see it – or don't?

When these four components become the structure of every agenda, clarity and consistency replace chaos. Receipts became the word that guided us. That word, receipt, became a measuring stick for our district's instructional integrity.

3. The People Behind the Practice

Every ILT has three types of people:

- **Truth Tellers:** Those who bring clarity.
- **Organizers:** Those who make things operational.
- **Story Tellers:** Those who measure impact and ensure sustainability.

When those roles overlap, the team becomes unstoppable, but the key is trust.

Without trust, the ILT becomes a courtroom. With trust, it becomes a classroom.

The superintendent doesn't lead every meeting; the vision creates its own followers. The principal doesn't have to dominate. The purpose should. A mature ILT becomes self-correcting because the framework has been internalized.

4. Leadership Presence and Process

The leader's job isn't to speak the most, it's to listen the best. Every ILT meeting is a temperature check of the culture. Here's the flow that we used districtwide:

1. **Open with Purpose.** Very first ILT, establish the why and say it all the time.
2. **Review the Data.** Not just the student data, but also the process data.
3. **Reflect on Progress.** Celebrate and/or coach.
4. **Plan Next Steps.** Set a success criterion and decide what will be done when success happens and when we fail to meet the standard.
5. **Onward or upward.** Data says we keep going or we celebrate and move on.

This rhythm turned meetings into ministry. People began to look forward to the ILT because it refueled, not drained them.

6. ILT as Professional Discipleship

The ILT is where adults are discipled in the discipline of clarity and leadership. It's where principals learn to share power, coaches learn to lead peers, and teachers learn that leadership is not a title but a trust.

Dr. Samuel DeWitt Proctor used to say that true preaching builds bridges between "the world that is and the world that ought to be." That's what the ILT does: it builds bridges between data and vision. When people start to see ILT as a place to solve problems and grow each other, transformation follows.

7. The Dangers of a Dysfunctional ILT

When ILTs drift, they often fall into three traps:

- **The Report Trap:** Meetings become information dumps instead of transformation hubs, and you never make it to monitor the action.
- **The Rescue Trap:** The principal's job is to protect them from the "Central Office", so he or she does all the talking while others nod and smile until it's over.
- **The Routine Trap:** Meetings happen because "Central Office" or "They Said" we must have them. Usually, in this scenario, the data is down. The adults believe it's the students' fault, or the district's fault, or a lack of resources. There is little to no interest in an ILT because no one believes that they are needed. Or, even worse, no one believes they can change it.

To avoid those traps, we introduced a simple mantra: "If it doesn't address our mission or vision, it doesn't belong on the agenda." That single filter saved hours and built trust in the integrity of the process. When they learned that it was about them and their adults and their students, and that we were going to do more than talk about it, but we would be about it, minds began to shift.

8. How to Keep the ILT Alive

The ILT stays alive through consistency. In each session, we tried to make sure that we stay focused on the fire and that we gathered to collect and discuss receipts. closed with two simple questions:

1. How do we know (receipts)?
2. What are we going to do because of the receipts?

Those two questions birthed accountability without anxiety. They reminded us that leadership isn't about perfection, it's about progress.

8. Application: Structuring Your ILT

Every effective ILT meeting should include the following elements:

Element	Description	Example
Vision	Our Why	"In order to effectively advance learning opportunities for all students…"
Purpose	Our What	"We are going to create a Learning University?"
Framework Integration	Which CRT-CM components are emphasized?	"System, Structure, and Process"
Action Steps	What will happen next, and who is responsible?	"Coach Smith will give the feedback about what we saw in the classroom on Wednesday. He will schedule a return visit at that time."

Monitoring Plan	How will progress be tracked?	"Based on our GBF data, we will use the engagement walkthrough form to visit these 9 teachers this week. Which three do you want to observe?"
Celebration Moment	What win can we acknowledge?	"We had 82% of the teachers use Think-Time I in observations last week. Our goal was 80%. What celebration did we promise & how are we going to acknowledge it in a respectful manner?"

How well does your team balance clarity with courage?

1. In what ways are you promoting voice to build capacity?
2. Do you enter the ILT with an aura of exhaustion or energy?
3. What would it take for your ILT to become your school's first exemplar of a "learning university"?

10. ILT Reflection Sheet — Implementation Focus

Question

Why?

What data reveals a fire that ILT needs to focus on?

What?

What specific actions will the ILT lead us to take?

How?

How will the ILT embed CRT-CM in each meeting?

How to address it?

How will you handle resistance, fatigue, and/or fear?

How to define success?

What outcomes will prove ILT impact?

How to communicate it?

How will you share the ILT purpose with staff?

How to measure it?

How will you evaluate consistency and engagement?

How will you celebrate it?

How will you acknowledge ILT victories?

Who will do all of this?

Closing Thought

The ILT is the heartbeat of every healthy school. When it beats with clarity, resources, training, coaching, and monitoring, the entire body thrives.

"The ILT will determine what lives and what dies in a building. What they, led by the Instructional Leader, tolerate, will be encouraged throughout the building. And what they won't tolerate, will not survive because there is power in the clarity, courage, commitment, and communication of the ILT."

Chapter 6

From Compliance to Culture: How Systems Grow Souls

1. The Trap of Compliance

Every great movement begins with relationships, then shifts to rules and always ends up coming back to relationships. Compliance is necessary for structure, but it's deadly when it becomes the goal and not a stop along the growth journey.

Too many districts, churches, and organizations mistake compliance for commitment. They think people's silence means alignment. They assume ticking boxes means transformation. But compliance is the floor, not the ceiling. Culture is the house you build on top of it. We learned that compliance would get you test results for a while, but culture gets you *life results*. Culture is when, as Lao Tzu said, "When the best leader's work is done, the people say, 'We did it ourselves'" Culture survives beyond the transformational leader. Culture is a bed of heart-shaped purple plants that grew in a valley of a mythical place. And when one ate of that heart-shaped herb, they became great. They became one with the ancestors and a protector of the present because it was their time to protect the kingdom of children that we have all decided to be a part of. When done well, ILT is not compliance. It is the Vibranium-heart of the school.

2. The Shift from Enforcing to Empowering

When I became superintendent, I walked into a system that had nice shiny things, but little passion for the sustained grind of success. The work done before me was great work. It was a part of the district's progression and growth. We were like the Gilded Gatsby. It was beautiful. It was real gold, but for it to be a part of who we are instead of a flash of what happened because of what we were forced to do, it had to be sustainable, and it had to be for more than students. Everyone in the district should be my focus, as the leader, wanting them to be the greatest. Every school had binders and social media pages of accolades, which were needed to change our mindset from good to great, but few people could articulate what the plans meant for students' futures. I realized then that compliance was blinding us. We were promoting being the best, but we were missing the real question of what happens after the news article. What happens to the students after graduation?

A chance encounter changed our perspective. One day, Dr. Lynne Hice and I were traveling from one school to another, and Dr. Hice, our former High School Principal, saw a young man whom she poured her soul into helping reach graduation. He was walking home with a huge bag of fast food for his family. Dr Hice asked him what happened to all the plans they had made for him after graduation. He shrugged and said life had taken him in a different direction. At that moment, we realized that our feeling of responsibility didn't stop at graduation. At that moment, we knew we had to change the focus.

Instead of celebrating one of the state's highest graduation rates, we began asking, *"What were students becoming other than graduates?"*

3. Culture Defined

Culture is the invisible curriculum. Culture is the thing that you will not tolerate in your organization. You cannot hide it. It permeates everything you do, and everyone knows the line. We defined culture as the collective agreement on what we believe, what we value, and what we will not tolerate.

Culture answers five questions:

1. Where do we spend our time?
2. Where do we place our resources?
3. What do we celebrate?
4. What do we coach?
5. What do we promote?

If you want to know a culture, watch what it refuses to ignore.

4. The CRT-CM Connection

Culture grows out of clarity, and clarity spreads through culture.
They feed one another.

- **Clarity** names what's important.
- **Resources** show what's valuable.
- **Training** reinforces expectations.
- **Coaching & Monitoring** sustain consistency.

Together, they create a cycle that transforms compliance into commitment and commitment into culture. A leader's greatest mistake is trying to create culture through command. You can't command belief. You cultivate it.

5. A Case Study: The Attendance Revival

Post-COVID, we had terrible chronic absenteeism. We sent letters, made calls, implemented policies, made videos, gave out ice cream, and even entered a parade with a car and signs championing school attendance. It moved it, but it didn't change it.

Then one school leadership team decided to treat attendance as a *culture* issue instead of a *compliance* issue.

- **Clarity:** Attendance is everyone's business.
- **Resources:** We put up scoreboards and celebrated classes and students with community-donated incentives.
- **Training:** School and district staff focused on a combined communication approach.
- **Coaching & Monitoring:** Weekly meetings reviewed attendance and celebrated improvement.

We replaced *threat letters* with *thank-you notes, positive phone calls, and social media posts* that celebrated improved attendance. In one semester, chronic absenteeism dropped to 9% and double digits for the year.

6. Building Culture Through Conversations

Culture isn't built through mandates. It's built through moments. In leadership, the most powerful words are not "Do this," but "why do this."

When leaders listen, trust grows.

When trust grows, culture changes.

In our district, I began transforming principal coaching meetings into wholesale "Instructional Leadership Team Meetings." I stopped waiting for Institute Days to talk to faculty and staff members about vision and our why. I started having those conversations at schools, with every school, at the classroom level.

Those small, sincere conversations did more for culture than any formal presentation ever could.

Because people don't remember what you say in PowerPoints, they remember how they felt when they accomplished something great for students, not because of what the district made them do. It's about each individual seeing themselves in the work.

7. The Spiritual Side of Culture

Culture is spirit made visible. Every organization has one. Some carry the spirit of excellence; others carry the spirit of exhaustion. The Bible says, *"Where the Spirit of the Lord is, there is liberty."* (2 Corinthians 3:17 NKJV)

That liberty isn't chaos; its clarity combined with responsibility. When people feel free to and know they are responsible to think, speak, and grow, culture breathes. The same is true for leadership. You can't have transformation without trust.

8. From Policy to Practice

Culture doesn't live in handbooks; it lives in habits. So, we started teaching our leaders to audit their *daily routines* through a cultural lens. We used Leverage Leadership by Dr. Paul Bambrick-Santoyo. In it, helped us to decide:

- What does my schedule communicate about what I value?
- How do I prioritize student and adult success?
- Am I inspecting what I am expecting and making adjustments?

Culture is not created by events but by action. All leader's actions are the walking embodiment of policy. Your actions are the manual your people read the most.

9. Application: The ILT as Culture Keepers

The ILT is the thermostat of a school. It doesn't just reflect the temperature; it sets it. To move from compliance to culture, the ILT must:

1. **Name the non-negotiables.** What will we no longer tolerate?
2. **Model the Mission.** How will we walk our talk?

3. **Narrate the Wins.** How will we celebrate our values in action?
4. **Nurture the People.** How will we protect and nurture the truth tellers and honor every voice while not succumbing to every idea?

10. Reflection Prompts

1. What current practices in your system reflect compliance instead of culture?
2. What does your team celebrate, and what does that reveal about your values?
3. How do you respond when someone violates expectations?
4. What would it look like to create a "revival of culture" in your workplace?
5. Who is the culture-carriers on your team, and how can you empower them?

11. ILT Reflection Sheet — Culture Focus

Question

Why?

What data reveals a need for cultural change?

What?

What cultural behaviors or attitudes must shift?

How?

How will the ILT model the desired culture?

How to address it?

How will you respond to cultural drift?

How to define success?

What evidence will show cultural growth?

How to communicate it?

How will you keep the message consistent?

How to measure it?

What indicators will track cultural health?

How will you celebrate it?

How will you honor people who reflect the new culture?

Who will do all of this?

Closing Thought

Compliance keeps order, but culture creates ownership. When people move from doing the work because they *must*, to doing it because they *believe in it*, that's when systems grow into a learning culture.

"Culture is the invisible curriculum; it teaches what the mission actually means."

Chapter 7

Measuring What Matters: Turning Data into Discipleship

1. Beyond the Numbers

In leadership, data is sacred, but only when it's used to reveal treasure and not used to make people feel cursed. Numbers tell a story but meaning and context give those numbers life. When leaders stop measuring what matters, they start managing what's easy.

Too often, data becomes a scoreboard instead of a mirror. Both are needed. We need scoreboards to tell us where we are, but in the words of famous National Football League Coach Dennis Greene, "They are who we thought they were!" Data is the mirror that tells us who we are at a moment in time, but it does not restrict us from becoming who we can become. We count test scores, attendance rates, and percentages, but we fail to count the development of who we become; the growth, the grit, the courageous grind behind them.

We had to learn that data doesn't drive people, purpose does. Data informs, but it doesn't often inspire. But when data meets discipleship, when the numbers are tied to names, the work becomes a calling.

2. The Purpose of Measurement

Measurement is not about control, it's about clarity. It asks, *"Are we becoming who we said we would be?"* Measurements are your ***receipts***!

If clarity defines the goal and training builds the skill, then measurement confirms the growth. Fidelity tells you if you are committed. Measurement tells you what impact your actions are having. You cannot have one without the other.

Every time I looked at a district dashboard, I reminded my team:

> "Behind every percentage point is a person. Behind every data point is a name."

Measurement matters most because it gives you clarity about impact.

3. The Dangers of Misused Data

Data, like most things in life, is neither good nor bad. It's how you use it.

I've seen leaders crush morale with metrics.

They present data like a verdict instead of a reflection of our ongoing practices.

When people fear the data, they start to manipulate it. When people trust the data, they start to multiply the clarity of the impact of adult behaviors. Know Thy Impact, as Dr. Jim Knight would say.

The difference lies in how the leader frames the picture or the lens you are looking through. Data doesn't need to be softer; we need to make the picture of what we are doing and why clearer. People should walk away saying, *"Now I understand where we are and how I can attack it to grow my students,"* not *"Now I understand that you look at my assessments to know how many students are in the red but never offer or ask me for solutions to improve things. Data is a gotcha."*

4. The CRT-CM Framework and Measurement

Measurement ties the entire CRT-CM Framework together:

- **Clarity** defines what success looks like.
- **Resources** ensure the tools exist to get there.
- **Training** equips people to reach it.
- **Coaching & Monitoring** verify that progress continues.

Measurement is the reflection that gives clarity to the impact of the process. It's how we know, with concrete clarity, what impact our action is having. *Does this do what we designed it to do or not?* Data is not the be-all and end-all to culture. However, real, measurable feedback during a change initiative often provides the critical mass needed to stay true to agreed-upon actions.

Every effective ILT asks, *"What evidence do I have that we are doing what we said we would do, and is what we're doing improving student achievement?"*

5. From Data Walls to Living Walls

I once visited a school where teachers had meticulously created a "data wall."

Every student's name was listed on colored cards by performance band. I thought it was the greatest thing I had ever seen. It was neat. It was color coordinated. It just made sense to me. I was in love. Then I began to realize that not all walls had the same expected maintenance. I began to go into buildings and ask teachers, "How often does this wall change?" Some said, "About three weeks ago." Others said, "About three months ago, when we took the last diagnostic." That's when I realized that while some of these data walls are not autopsy reports like we used to get when I was at the high school (autopsy meaning, the data is about students we no longer have; we can do nothing about it). But just like anything else in a building, nothing changes at a school unless the instructional leader puts the right structures in place to move them and how often. Bottom line, it's a culture of expectation set by the leader.

By the time I became Assistant Superintendent of Curriculum & Instruction, we didn't use physical data walls. We started a system of assessment that included scheduled common formative assessments (CFAs), quarterly benchmark assessments, and a once-every-three-months diagnostic. Based on these structures, schools updated student progress every week in some schools and every three weeks, at most, at elementary schools, and every 4.5 weeks at a minimum in secondary schools.

Data headed northeast on a data chart brought teachers alive. When they became energized and the collective efficacy grew, the people at the school took full ownership of their student data. It was no longer the district data. It was their data from their students and their efforts in and outside the classroom.

6. Turning Data into Discipleship

Data without discipleship is like the verbal Kool-Aid that Jim Jones served. Discipleship without data is shallow. Only when they are combined do we get the gift of real feedback and evidence of a coming transformation that's not built on a program, but on a sustainable process led by the experts, the people in the building.

Discipleship asks:

- Is the residue of consistency present? Are we doing what we said we would do?
- Are we shaping both collective and individual efficacy as we form habits?
- Are we measuring outcomes in the context of why we say we are doing this work?

When Jesus sent the seventy disciples out, He told them to return and *"rejoice that their names are written in heaven."* (Luke 10:20 NKJV) Even He, "Jesus," was tracking impact. We keep it on an Excel workbook; Jesus keeps it in the Book of Life.

In the Learning University, measurement becomes discipleship when it's used to *affirm progress, adjust practice,* and *honor effort.*

7. Building a Measurement System That Honors People

Here's how our district restructured its approach:

1. **Define the Right Metrics.** You will have many fires. There will be many things we can work on. When you identify the problem, define the key measurable adult behaviors, and commit to a clear picture of student success, you have a plan. None of this can happen without clarity about the correct metrics. Remember, it's about what you are doing, how you plan on doing it, and why it drives it, but you must have clarity on how it will be measured.

2. **Visualize Progress.** Have a scoreboard. You need a public scoreboard, so targeted stakeholders know what the goal is and where you stand. You need a private scoreboard to hold you accountable for monitoring success. Scoreboards and dashboards not only show your scores, but I promise you that they tell a story, your story.

3. **Celebrate Incremental Wins.** You don't set goals to say, *Gotcha Ya!* You set goals so that every week, every month, every quarter, every CFA, every diagnostic, every day a student shows up, every time we find adults performing phenomenal, culture-based actions, we need to celebrate, but there is nothing to celebrate without the courage to say what we want. The goal is that hopefully a courageous act of saying publicly that you are bearing yourself before this community. I am working towards a goal, and either I

made it or I didn't. Make no mistake: I am focused on the prize, and the prize is defined by the goal.

4. **Share Transparently.** Put up a public dashboard. Put up a declaration in the hallway of what the 5th-grade math goal is. Put on social media the attendance goal, and talk about the culture goals to students, even when they are visiting the principal's office for correction. Be transparent so that everyone knows what you hope to accomplish. Yes, put the pressure on yourself because it is not a goal for clicks or likes. It is a goal to understand how well a group of professionals can pull a plan together that is strong enough to support the needs of their students. Be unapologetically optimistic about the impact you plan on making.

5. **Reflect Spiritually.** When you have open and honest data meetings, they should start with your why. Why am I an educator? Why am I in this seat? Why am I serving the children of this school? Why won't I tolerate anything less than this team's best effort, not like a superman or superwoman, but as a group of people clear about who they are, where they are, what they want to do, why they want to do it, and why? Why, the foundation.

That last question changed the atmosphere of our conversations. We began using that question to begin our very first ILT of the year. It changed our meetings from compliance torture sessions for the schools to impactful, truth-telling, leader-growing moments designed to heal and grow, not wound and hurt.

8. Application: The ILT Data Cycle

Each ILT should build a **Data Cycle** that mirrors this process:

1. **Clarity & Collect:** Gather accurate, timely data that is a receipt for the ILT focus.
2. **Analyze:** Look for trends, not outliers, that may be an area that we can address to change how adults are instructing students.
3. **Interpret:** So what? Discuss what the data means, not just what it says.
4. **Plan:** What are we going to do and how do we do it? Decide on at least one specific goal, one action step, one data collection tool, and decide on the through line.
5. **Monitor:** Inspect what you expect. Get receipts on the fidelity of the implementation of the plan.
6. **Coach:** Coaches don't just yell and fuss. They encourage too. Based on what you find when you and your team monitor, at your coaches' meeting (ILT), pick out people that need to be coached and who will coach them. Pick out people who need to be celebrated.
7. **Celebrate:** Acknowledge people's hard work and consistency both publicly and personally. And it is not based on some feel-good, everybody gets a trophy jazz. It is based on the concrete goals that you set in the first four phases of the ILT. You were transparent upfront letting people know not only what the expected goal was, but you were also transparent about the steps to get to success and the goal line that we must reach to reach success. When people score a touchdown, celebrate like somebody from the state of

Alabama, the Saturday after Thanksgiving. (IYKYK 😀)

9. Reflection Prompts

1. What are you currently measuring that doesn't matter, and what matters that you're not measuring? Who decided what mattered? Who communicated it?
2. How can you make data conversations feel like opportunities instead of obligations?
3. When was the last time your team celebrated progress, not perfection?
4. How does your current system ensure data is like a medical round, that drives practices on live patients, and not like an autopsy, a look at children that are gone?
5. What story is your data talking about your culture?

10. ILT Reflection Sheet — Measurement Focus

Question

Why?

What data trends require deeper reflection?

What?

What metrics best capture what matters most?

How?

How will you collect and share data meaningfully?

How to address it?

How will you respond if data doesn't show growth?

How to define success?

What short- and long-term indicators matter most?

How to communicate it?

How will you tell the story behind the numbers?

How to measure it?

What tools ensure data accuracy and integrity?

How will you celebrate it?

How will you honor the people behind the progress?

Who will do all of this?

11. The Superintendent's Reflection

Leadership demands reality. It demands accountability. It demands clarity of purpose. But if you are asking people to perform as if they are disciples to a mission and not an employee looking for a paycheck, it requires a clarity of purpose and an honest introspective look at why you do what you do. Leadership is about being what people need to be their highest and truest self so they can do the will or the goal of the organization. In education, the goal is to keep children safe and educate them. In the church, it is to carry out the Great Commission and preach the Gospel; Repent, the Kingdom of Heaven is at hand. In both situations, how you define success is important. How you track your impact is integrity. When you measure what matters, you make ministry measurable. That's when numbers start preaching.

> **"Data is not the grade; it's the feedback to guide action."**

Conclusion

Becoming the University: Where Learning Never Stops

1. The Journey from System to Soul

When this work began, we were trying to fix people. At first, everyone said it was the students. So, we pursued student engagement, and it helped. Then, we decided that if we focused on teacher pedagogy and increased their knowledge of both pedagogy and curriculum, done with embedded professional development, we would win the proverbial prize. We got a coach for every school. We got a coach for the coaches (Tip of the hat to Jackie Flowers), every principal got a coach, and the superintendent even got a coach. The best thing we did was geta structure and a process that helped guide us to a definition of what good pedagogy is. Get Better Faster by Paul Bambrick-Santoyo and Jon Saphier became our base for defining good pedagogy. Until you know how you define good pedagogy, if you don't have a common definition of it, and you are facing a challenging student achievement situation, you will never gain the traction of everyone using the same language and pulling in the same direction. I digress.

After we "fixed" pedagogy, while that helped some, it didn't take us to the level that we felt we should be. Then we made a massive investment in curriculum materials and professional development for teachers in the use of the curriculum. Fixing the curriculum system (thanks Lynne Hice & Jill Edwards).

We thought that if we wrote better plans, produced better reports, and held tighter meetings, everything would fall into place.

What we learned after everything was fixed is this: you can major in 1,000 things, but unless you are clear on why you're doing the work, what you are doing, and how you are doing it, the work will never truly land. What I mean by how is:

- How are you going to do it?
- How will you communicate it/roll it out?
- How will you define success?
- How will you measure it?
- How long do you expect it to take to meet the success criteria?
- How will you address coaching & feedback?
- How will you check the progress collectively?
- How will you celebrate wins & celebrate success?
- How will you divide the work? (Who will do what/through line? Who owns it?)

Deming says, *A bad system will beat a good person every time.* We don't have time to experiment with creating systems from the ground up. Every district is different, but without systems, structures, and processes, the lift will always be heavier than it should; doubt will always gnaw at efficacy, and success will always look like a mystery. Systems allow people to do what they are best at, be efficient at moving heaven and earth to reach clear, hairy, audacious goals that they will reach one step at a time.

Clarity, Resources, Training, Coaching, and Monitoring are not bureaucratic boxes to check; they are human disciplines that lead to the formation of instructional leaders and surgically, strategically educated children. They are spiritual acts of leadership that teach us how to see, to serve, and to sustain.

At the heart of it all, leadership isn't about control; it's about service. It is about working in fields first cultivating and then harvesting fruit that is student learning, and therefore the sweet fruit of student success, cultivated by the human cycle of discipleship called CRT-CM.

During my second year of being a teacher and coach, pouring my life and soul into helping other people's children be successful and safe, I had a young nephew. He was a local track and basketball star from a small, rural school. I loved him, but like most of my life, I was always busy. He was trying to get a scholarship educational career. I helped him look up a few places to try out, but I did not take the time to really look at his problem. Instead, I gave him some good solutions that should lead to a happy ending of a scholarship or at least he would end up as a gym rat manager who, if he ever got his shot, would surely make the team. But that is not how it turned out. He had a car accident traveling home from a tryout. I was devastated but never remotely close to being as devastated as my sister. As I look back on that moment, it made me realize what type of educator I would be. In that moment, I knew that never again was solutionism going to be my main way of handling problems. Never would I treat a child like a student. They are somebody's child. I never got a chance to help my nephew become more successful than he already was. He was a good-looking, athletic disciple of Christ that God wanted with Him. My take away from it was to make sure that I helped every child who was under my umbrella of influence to be successful. I found out that the only way to do that is to help adults be cared for, equipped, and cultivated to be a success, so they could do the same for our students. I then learned that without systems, structures, processes grounded in a deeply rooted and grounded why, nothing would change. My final lesson to learn was that the central office can't do it alone. The principal can't do it alone. But an instructional team of adults is committed to the success and safety of all children.

Success in a school has a name. It's called **Learning.**

2. The University Within

When I talk about the Learning University, I'm not describing a building. I'm describing a culture where the very act of learning is at the center of what everyone is striving to learn. The Learning University is the place where everyone is both a teacher and a student. Where everyone must learn and lead. Where mistakes are not monuments of failure but milestones that, because we put in the work, we can say with a clear conscience that we know that does not work here and here is why. There is nothing wrong with our students or us. We just must try the next strategy. Every failure is a lesson.

It's the culture where a custodian's insight matters as much as a consultant. Where a principal's humility and sacrifice teach more than a PowerPoint ever could. Where growth is not seasonal. It is a perennial product that we expect to harvest every day, every quarter, every semester, every year.

When learning becomes identity, not activity, the entire building breathes, moves, thinks, and acts with purpose.

3. From Transaction to Transformation

There are many ways to lead, but there are three that seem to be the most common in education and government. You can be a transactional leader doing it for what you can get out of it. You can be a transformational leader that transforms an organization to something more and other than it was. The third is to lead by serving with the goal that those that you lead become more, as Dr. Greenleaf would say, autonomous, more likely themselves to serve and then lead. The servant leader not only wants the organization to transform, but the servant leader desires that each member of the team; students, parents, faculty, staff, administrators, board members, community, while under their organizational umbrella becomes their highest and truest self, or, at the least is honest enough to say where they currently are and where they currently are is not where they want to be.

You can manage transactions, you can lead transformation, but only a servant leader can steward the gifts that he or she has been given by God, the Creator, in order to set up a culture of everyone can get better because everyone can learn to be their highest and truest selves in order to edify the body of people that they serve and serve with, both are one and the same.

At First Missionary Baptist Church, I often tell my congregation: "Don't get religion and miss the opportunity to have a relationship with God through Christ Jesus."

Don't get the job and make it about keeping the job. Just being on the team is not enough. You accepting salvation from Christ will get you on the team, but Christ didn't die for you to be on the team. Christ came for us to help spread the Gospel; Repent! The Kingdom of Heaven is at hand! To be more like Jesus, we have to be real about what we are and what we are not. It is through the system of Jesus Christ that we learn what to be: a child of God. It is through the structure of the two ordinances of the Bible and the Great Commission that we find the structure of what we are supposed to be doing, going to baptize, teach, and make disciples, and remember Christ's death, burial, and resurrection with His Holy Communion.

4. The Legacy of Clarity

As I look back, I realize that everything starts and ends with clarity. Clarity is not just the first step of the framework; it's the language of a culture that is serious about growing and learning.

When a leader is clear, this gives the rest of the team confidence and courage. When a leader is confused, the people perish for a lack of vision.

Clarity gives purpose a red-dot target to focus on. Clarity allows you to set aside all theory and wondering and debating and pick up clearly articulated goals, see what measurable adult actions are happening and how this is impacting our clearly articulated goal.

My prayer is that you never let the fog of urgency and panic lead you to wreck and miss the stated purpose for which all the hours of meetings, practicing, collaboration, missed planning periods, and early morning meetings were spent to reach a purpose that panic made you lose sight of.

Pause long enough to ask:

- What are we really trying to accomplish?

- Who can clearly articulate their role in carrying out this goal?

- Why do we believe we do this work, and why do we believe this work is worth doing?

If you can answer those three questions with honesty, you're already halfway to transformation.

5. The Circle Keeps Turning

The CRT-CM Framework ends where it began: with a circle.

Because leadership, like faith, is continuous.

You will never "arrive" at mastery. You can master a level. When that happens, in my experience, God will level you up to the next level to do His will on the next level. We are continually being formed and transformed by Christ. We are continually being transformed into the best tool that we can be to serve God by serving people. So, every day that you are alive, you have a chance to learn and get better. Every disappointing result we get is the beginning of an opportunity for a group of adults to use systems, structures, and processes to look at what is best for student safety and learning, and put that plan into play with clarity, resource allocation, training, and using the twin accountability partners of monitoring and coaching.

That's why I call it Seeking Learning University, not Found Learning University.

The journey takes you where it takes you. The reality is, we have no control over our journey. We never know when we are facing the very situation that may change the world. Every day we lead, teach, and learn in a cycle. We owe it to the people we serve and the God we serve to seek to learn and create a culture of learning to seek God's wisdom, grace, and approval.

6. The Spiritual Charge

The prophet Habakkuk wrote, "Write the vision, and make it plain." (Habakkuk 2:2 NKJV)

That's what this whole work has been about, making it plain. Not easy, not glamorous, but plain enough that everyone can run with it. Give the people clarity of purpose.

Leadership is not for the faint of heart. It's for those who can pray in the dark and not flinch in the dark because they know that God is with them. For those who know that being in charge is not about them, it is about doing what is pleasing in God's sight, despite those who may not like what you are doing. Don't ride the fence. Be clear about what you want. To do that, tell them what you're going to tell them. Tell them. Then, tell them what you told them. Leaders, keep:

- Keep writing the vision.

- Keep speaking the vision.

- Keep making it plain.

- Keep believing that every interaction you have with your people is a chance to shed light on the dark corner that holds the latest rumor.

The vision makes the invisible visible; it gives sight to the blind. Keep valuing every opportunity to show people the vision and use words when necessary.

Because the goal is to create a system of learning for youth and adults that will create such a culture of learning that everyone grows into their highest and truest selves to address student learning. Keep the faith!

7. My Benediction to Leaders

If I could stand before you like I stand before my congregation, this is what I'd say:

- May you never mistake work for ministry.
- May your meetings become classrooms of clarity and understanding.
- May you measure what matters and communicate why it matters.
- May you resource what's right, not just what's equal.
- May your training steady hearts and skyrocket dreams.
- May your coaching restore confidence, and your monitoring affirm it.

And when the weight of leadership feels too heavy, may you remember that you are a part of the Kingdom, but you are not the King. If the King calls you to serve, He will equip you until your time of service there is over. Then, the next level.

You are not just a superintendent, a central office leader, an instructional coach, a principal or assistant principal, counselor, clerk, custodian, or teacher. You are a tool of the Chief Architect, and He is using you to build belief, steward souls, and cultivate minds for the success of everyone's futures.

The work is sacred. The framework is simple. And the university? It's already inside you.

8. Final Reflection

We are all students in God's school of leadership. We are all leaders in His army of saints who are being formed to edify the rest of His Holy Army.

I had the good fortune of earning an A on our district report card twice during my tenure. The grade did something for my resume. It made everyone know that yes, our students can learn too. Our students are smart, and our adults are capable. But it is not the awards that mean you have a Learning University. It is grace, grit, tears, speaking truth to power, and growth by a critical mass that is the true residue or evidence, or, my personal favorite, the receipts that you have a true Learning University.

Seeking Learning University: One Leader's Way of Pursuing Clarity Through Instructional Leadership Team (ILT) Meetings

by Dr. Jimmy D. Shaw Jr.

Appendices

Appendix A — ILT Reflection Sheet (Full Template)

Guiding Question

Why?

What statistical data led you to this? What is your fire?

What?

What are you going to do?

How?

What are your strategies, structures, and supports?

How to address it?

How will you respond if progress stalls?

How to define success?

What evidence will show you've achieved your goal?

How to communicate it?

How will you ensure all staff understand the plan?

How to measure it?

What tools and timelines will you use to check progress?

How will you celebrate it?

What wins will you honor and how?

Who will do all of this?

Which people or roles carry each responsibility?

Tip: The ILT Reflection Sheet should live and breathe.
Don't fill it once and file it away—revisit it monthly as a mirror for your progress and alignment.

Appendix B — CRT-CM Framework Planning Template

CRT-CM = Clarity + Resources + Training (surrounded by Coaching & Monitoring)

Use this framework to anchor every plan, project, or initiative.

Component	Guiding Question	Your Plan
C - Clarity	What exactly are we trying to accomplish? What is our "why"?	
R - Resources	What tools, people, and supports do we need to make this happen?	
T – Training	What professional learning or capacity building is needed? Who needs to be trained and by when?	
Coaching & Monitoring (Circle)	How will we observe, guide, and sustain progress continuously? What feedback loops will we maintain?	

Visual Reminder:

- Triangle = C, R, T at each point
- Circle = Continuous Coaching & Monitoring surrounding the triangle
- Color Palette = *Electric Blue and Silver*

Appendix C

Purpose and Desired Outcomes

Purpose:

In order to effectively advance learning and opportunities for all students to achieve and grow, we will create a Learning University at the district and school levels that has a clear standard for what happens in a teaching and learning culture by focusing on model practices that can be implemented, replicated, assessed, and monitored with district and school teams—with outcomes driven by:

- Culture: What we won't tolerate.
- Practice: What we want to see happening.
- Student Achievement: The ultimate measure of how what happened impacted students.

Desired Outcomes:

- Advance how we build capacity in school leadership teams (Principals, APs, Coaches).
- Establish exemplars of effective ILT practice.
- Strengthen the through-line between adult behavior and student success:

Principal → AP → Coaches → ALs → Teachers → Students

- Ensure every adult in the system sees themselves as part of the vision.

Appendix D
About the Author

Dr. Jimmy D. Shaw, Jr.

Superintendent, Florence City Schools

Pastor, First Missionary Baptist Church of Tuscumbia, Alabama

Dr. Shaw is a lifelong learner and servant-leader whose journey bridges the classroom, the pulpit, and the community. As a retired superintendent from Alabama, he championed a culture of doing what was best for students, innovation, and clarity in leadership.

At First Missionary Baptist Church of Tuscumbia, he shepherds a congregation steeped in history and hope, emphasizing a gospel that educates as much as it elevates.

A native of Florence, AL, Dr. Shaw believes leadership is both privilege and passion. It is an act of worship and obedience to Christ through working for Him and His Kingdom. His CRT-CM Framework and Learning University philosophy have become guiding tools for transforming systems through spiritual, cultural, and instructional renewal.

He is the devoted husband of Felicia Shaw, father of Jayden, Jacob, and Caleb, and son of Sarah Shaw and the late Jimmy Davis Shaw, Sr.

He dedicates this work to his Lord and Savior, Jesus Christ, his family, all his fellow servants in education, the foxhole friends, and his First Missionary Baptist Church Family, who daily remind him that God has called him for such a time as this. Therefore, love God and love people.